·SUPERBOOK·

BALLET

CATHERINE DELL

Kingfisher Books

Contents

Kingfisher Books, Grisewood & Dempsey Ltd,
Elsley House, 24–30 Great Titchfield Street,
London W1P 7AD

This revised edition published in 1986 by Kingfisher Books
Originally published in 1979 in hard cover by the Hamlyn Publishing
Group as *Ballet Dancing*
10 9 8 7 6 5 4

British Library Cataloguing-in-Publication Data.
A catalogue record for this book is available from the British Library

ISBN 0-86272-196-2

Cover design by Terry Woodley
Cover illustration by Diana Bowles / *John Martin & Artists Ltd*
Phototypeset by Southern Positives and Negatives (SPAN), Lingfield, Surrey
Printed in Hong Kong

Ballet

Great companies – from the Ballets Russes and the Bolshoi to Martha Graham and the Dance Theater of Harlem; famous and dazzling impresarios, choreographers and dancers – from Nijinsky, Pavlova and Diaghilev to Ashton, Cranko and Nureyev; superb music – from the 'Romantic' classics of Tchaikovsky and the daring of Stravinsky to such great 'moderns' as Bernstein and Khachaturin: the world of ballet is full of immense versatility and fascination. Yet it is a fleeting world. Ballet and dance are perhaps the most transitory of all the arts – despite film and television. And photographs and words cannot fully convey the 'feel' and nuances of ballet.

In this book the author has successfully captured something of the magic of this great art. She unfolds the story of ballet from the formal dance of the French court to the lively movements of today. She tells us how a dancer is trained, from the first steps to the first solo performance on stage. She describes the movements of ballet with helpful drawings and examples of the movements from actual ballets. She explains how a ballet is made, from the choreographers' idea through to the first night.

The word Ballet comes from the Italian *ballare*, meaning, literally, 'to dance', and it was first used to describe elaborate music, dance and mime shows put on for the nobility of Europe. Over the centuries, the ballet remained an entertainment performed in the luxurious surroundings of royal courts and magnificent opera houses. Only in the 20th century has ballet reached a wide public, as famous dancers began to tour the world with their companies.

In recent years, film and television have had a great affect on the popularity of dance as a form of entertainment. Both classical ballet and modern dance have become familiar to many people. The techniques of modern dance have also influenced classical ballet. As modern companies such as the Martha Graham company and the Ballet Rambert have explored new styles, so traditional ballet has come to include some of their techniques.

Dance today is an exciting and varied entertainment, involving many different styles and personalities.

▶ **Dame Alicia Markova rehearsing Caroline Humpston for Markova's revival of Fokine's *Les Sylphides* for the London Festival Ballet. Dame Alicia Markova was one of the English dancers in Diaghilev's Ballets Russes. She later formed her own company with another English dancer from the Ballets Russes, Anton Dolin.**

◀ **Flemming Flindt, the great Danish dancer and choreographer created the ballet *Triumph of Death* for the Royal Danish Ballet to perform on television and later on stage.**

The Story of Ballet

In Italy 500 years ago the nobility entertained important visitors with elaborate pageants of poetry, music, mime and dancing. When an Italian, Catherine de Medici, married Henry II of France, she introduced this kind of pageant to the French court. One of Catherine's most dazzling entertainments was the *Ballet Comique de la Reine* produced in 1581 to celebrate her sister's marriage. So, thanks to Catherine de Medici, ballets, as these festivities were called, became a feature of French court life. They reached their peak of popularity almost a hundred years later in the reign of Louis XIV.

Ballet was eventually taken over by professional dancers and consisted mainly of singing and dancing. At first all dancers were men but by the end of the 17th century women were dancing. One of the most famous was Marie

▲ The *Ballet Comique de la Reine,* Paris 1581. This sumptuous entertainment, which took place in the great hall of the royal palace, told the story of Circe, an enchantress, who turned men into animals. Like all court ballets it included singing and acting as well as dancing. In the *Ballet Comique* (*comique* means dramatic, not funny) the Queen and her ladies took part in the dancing.

▶ This painting by the French artist Edgar Degas (1834–1917), shows dancers in a studio at the Paris Opéra. The Opéra was founded by Louis XIV. It has its own school which ranks as the oldest ballet school in the world. The dancers in the picture are wearing romantic-style costumes introduced by Marie Taglioni.

Camargo who caused a sensation by shortening her skirt and wearing flat shoes so that she could do simple jumps.

In the late 1700s Jean-Georges Noverre, a choreographer, revolutionized ballet. He believed that dancing should be more than meaningless movement: it should tell a story. He did away with singing and the wearing of masks and made the dancers use mime and facial expressions.

The 19th century brought more changes. *La Sylphide* (1832), instead of being about classical heroes and heroines, as most ballets were, told the tragic story of a forest sprite who fell in love with a mortal. *La Sylphide* was the first great Romantic ballet. For dancing, like the other arts, had come under the spell of the Romantic movement, which exalted emotion, imagination and the supernatural.

The Romantic movement in dancing lasted barely 20 years. Ballet then went into decline. But not in Russia. The Imperial Ballet companies in St Petersburg and Moscow were

▲ Marie Taglioni moved with amazing lightness. Her father, who trained her, once said: "If I heard my daughter dance, I would kill her".

renowned for their superb productions. Many French dancers and choreographers travelled to Russia to work, among them Marius Petipa who went there in 1847.

In Russia, Petipa choreographed over 60 ballets. Each ballet contained important dances for the *corps de ballet* (chorus), brilliant *variations* (solos) for the principal dancers and at least one grand *pas de deux* (duet). Petipa worked closely with both dancers and composers; with Tchaikóvsky he created three of the world's best-loved ballets: *Sleeping Beauty*, *Nutcracker* and *Swan Lake*.

By the end of the century Petipa was considered old-fashioned. A new revolution began, led by a Russian: Diaghilev.

Serge Diaghilev was a St Petersburg law student who gave up his studies to edit an art magazine. He and his friends were full of exciting ideas and wanted to try them out. They decided to go to Paris. Diaghilev treated Paris to Russian music and opera and in 1909 to Russian ballet.

Diaghilev brought his audiences the best: top dancers from the imperial companies –

► Anna Pavlova in *The Dying Swan,* a solo created for her by Fokine. *The Dying Swan* became Pavlova's symbol. Wherever she danced audiences marvelled at her sensitive portrayal of the bird's anguish.

◄ Vaslav Nijinsky's most famous part was the title role in Fokine's *The Spirit of the Rose (Spectre de la Rose).* He is dancing with Tamara Karsavina. Nijinsky's costume, made of pink rose petals, frequently had to be renewed, because admirers took the petals as souvenirs.

▼ A scene from the London Festival Ballet's production of *The Three Cornered Hat,* originally one of the Ballets Russes's many triumphs.

among them Pavlova, Karsavina and Nijinsky – as well as new ballets. Parisian ballet-goers found the productions breath-taking. Never before had they seen such superb dancing. In 1911, Diaghilev formed his own company: *Les Ballets Russes*.

The Ballets Russes owes its enormous fame to Diaghilev's genius for discovering and exploiting talent. He employed choreographers such as Fokine, Nijinsky, Massine and Balanchine, and dancers like Marie Rambert, Ninette de Valois and Serge Lifar. Composers included Stravinsky and Debussy, and his designers some of the most famous artists of the century.

Diaghilev gave the world a treasury of great ballets: Fokine's *Firebird, Les Sylphides, Petrushka*: Nijinsky's *L'Après Midi d'un Faune*; Massine's *The Three Cornered Hat*; Balanchine's *The Prodigal Son*.

When Diaghilev died, the Ballets Russes broke up. Marie Rambert had already gone to London. She was followed by Ninette de Valois, Alicia Markova and Anton Dolin. Marie Rambert founded a dancing school, Ninette de Valois also founded a company, the Vic-Wells which became Britain's Royal Ballet. George Balanchine went to America where he founded the New York City Ballet.

Martha Graham (right) with members of her company in *Phaedra*, a story from Greek mythology.

The New Dance

Americans were leading the way in modern dance. Isadora Duncan was born in San Francisco in 1878. She loved dancing but hated ballet: she found it artificial. She believed in spontaneous movement and used to dance barefoot. Her ideas inspired Martha Graham, a fellow American. In the 1930s and 1940s Martha Graham developed a new dance system. Her technique makes great use of the dancer's back; it also includes angular, twisted body shapes, falls and floor movements.

Today's ballet scene is full of variety. There are long story ballets; there are also more and more one-act ballets. Some tell a story but many short ballets are abstract. Balanchine, in particular, was famous for his abstract works. Mostly they are pure-dance works: movements added to music, without a trace of time or place.

◄ Béjart's company in
his version of *Rite of Spring,* a
ballet created for Nijinsky and
which caused an uproar at its
first night in 1913 because it
was so unconventional.

Abstraction goes well with modern dance,
and many modern-dance choreographers concentrate on ballets without stories. They often
experiment with revolutionary ideas in sound,
lighting and costume and scenery. The results
can be sensational.

Dance reaches large audiences through the
cinema and television. Many filmed ballets are
actual stage productions. Some are set up in a
studio and filmed there, and a few are created
especially for the screen, like *The Red Shoes,*
starring Robert Helpman and Moira Shearer,
and the Royal Ballet's exquisite *Tales of Beatrix
Potter.*

► Musicals on stage and screen often include
dance sequences, ranging from the elegant
footwork of an old Fred Astaire movie to the fast-
moving body-rhythms of *West Side Story.* The
exciting dance movements were arranged by
Jerome Robbins who also choreographed *The
King and I* and *Fiddler on the Roof.*

Left: Dancers of the Ballet Rambert in *Cruel Garden,* a full-length dance spectacle based on the life and work of the Spanish poet, Garcia Lorca. The Ballet Rambert is Britain's oldest ballet company, brainchild of Dame Marie Rambert, one of the most remarkable figures in the world of dance.

Learning Ballet

Learning to dance is hard work. It also takes a long time. Proper ballet training generally starts at the age of 11 and takes place in a special school. To get into a ballet school children have to pass an audition and an interview. The audition is taken as a class where pupils do basic exercises. The examiners are concerned with the candidates' sense of rhythm and their shape: their feet, arms, legs, back and knees. At the interviews, which are held individually, the examiners are still assessing the child's size and shape; they are also looking for an alert mind.

Ballet school is in many ways similar to any other school. Pupils do ordinary lessons and study for the usual exams. In addition, they learn ballet every day, except Sunday. There are other special lessons, such as music, drama, singing, national dancing and the history of dance.

Is such a crowded timetable really necessary? Does a dancer need to know about

A junior class at the Stuttgart ballet school. When children join a ballet school at 10 or 11 they have usually had four or five years of dancing lessons. The choice of teacher for these first lessons is vitally important, as a bad teacher can do life-long damage in just a few months. Many children with talent have had to give up dancing their feet having been ruined by bad training.

11

For the performance staged at the end of term, pupils have to learn how to cut, fit and sew costumes. Here girls at the Bush Davies School in London (one of Britain's leading ballet schools) are busy making costumes for their production. Costumes are always made to measure; they must be an exact fit to allow the dancers to move freely.

At end of term shows pupils display their new skills. As well as dancing, these involve making costumes, painting scenery and wearing stage make-up. Schools attached to major companies sometimes offer more exciting opportunities. For instance, when the Royal Danish Ballet puts on its most popular production, *Napoli*, children from the company's school form part of the festive crowd in the final act.

At 16, most young people in ballet school face an important decision. Should they leave and say goodbye to dance, or, if they are good enough, stay on for a further two years? The final stage of training is rigorous, and only the keenest students can survive the pace. There is no longer time for general studies. The whole day (seven or eight hours) is given over to dance: national dancing, historical dancing, tap-dancing, modern stage dancing, Martha Graham style dance, mime, drama, stage make-up, costume, choreography, notation, music – and ballet proper. The daily class – still consisting of *barre* work and centre practice – now lasts longer, and there are special lessons for *pas de deux* (dancing with a partner), *tour de force* (advanced steps) and for teaching.

By the time they leave ballet school, students normally have a teacher's certificate and have gained some teaching experience by taking beginners' classes on Saturdays. Some students genuinely want to teach, but for the majority the qualification is a kind of insurance: something to fall back on if they do not succeed as a dancer or to retire to when their dancing career is over.

In their last year at ballet school, students look for a place with a company. Finding one is not easy: as many as 300 may audition for just one place! Only a few lucky ones get into top companies; even fewer will become top dancers. The five-year old at dancing class may dream of life as a new Fonteyn or Nureyev; the chances of that dream coming true are remote.

algebra, amoeba and atmospheric pressure? No, but then only a few ballet learners – perhaps only one in ten – actually become dancers. Some give up because they have to: maybe they have grown too large or too tall. Others give up because by the time they are 16 they are no longer as enthusiastic about dancing as they once were. The fact that they have learnt mathematics, English and history makes it possible for them to change direction and go into other careers. A few put their ballet training to good use, but not as dancers: classes in drama and stagecraft are a good stepping stone for an acting career; graceful movement is an ideal preparation for modelling.

What to Wear

For dancing, clothing must be simple, comfortable and easily washed. Normally girls dress in short tunics or leotards with cotton socks when they are young, and tights when they are older. Boys wear socks, footless tights and T-shirts.

Everybody, once they start intensive ballet training, uses leg-warmers. These woolly stockings may look unromantic but they are essential – especially at the beginning of a class or rehearsal – as they keep the leg muscles warm and flexible.

Shoes are vitally important. At first children wear flats – soft leather or satin shoes with unblocked (ordinary) toes. When girls are ready to dance on *pointe*, they change over to blocked shoes, with square, solid toes that help them to balance.

▲ Students practising a folk dance. National dancing is an important part of ballet training as many works feature dances from different countries.

▼ For students at Britain's Royal Ballet School, the highlight of the year is their performance at the Royal Opera House, Covent Garden. Here Royal Ballet students are dancing in *Les Patineurs (The Skaters)*.

A lesson in stage make-up at Perm choreographic school. Perm, an industrial city in the USSR became closely associated with ballet in 1941 when the Kirov Company was evacuated there.

Senior students in class. Along the studio wall, behind the *barre,* is a long full-length mirror. Mirrors are important: they allow dancers to watch themselves and so correct any faulty step.

Final-year students from the Bolshoi school in *Les Sylphides.* This short plotless ballet was created by Fokine in 1908 as an examination piece for the Imperial Ballet School in St Petersburg. It was then called *Chopiniana* (in honour of its music, by Chopin).

Ballet Steps

Posture This means standing as tall as possible with the hips directly over the feet, the back pulled straight and all the muscles pulled upwards to give the body a slim line.

Turn-out The legs should be turned out from the hips so that the toes point sideways. Turn-out adds beauty to the line of the body.

Positions of the feet Pierre Beauchamp, Louis XIV's dancing master, first worked out the five positions of the feet. These positions are the starting and finishing point of all steps.

Positions of the arms In all five positions, the shoulders are kept down; the elbows are rounded to create a flowing line right through the arms to the finger tips.

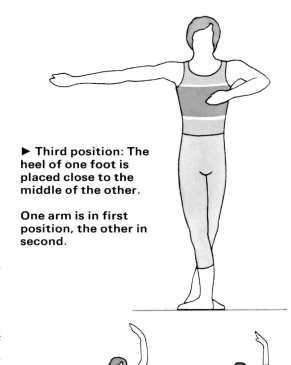

▶ **Third position: The heel of one foot is placed close to the middle of the other.**

One arm is in first position, the other in second.

▲ **First position: The heels are together and both feet are completely turned out to form a single straight line.**

The arms are raised in front of the body and delicately curved.

▲ **Second position: The heels of the turned-out feet are about 30 cm (12 in) apart.**

The arms, sloping from the shoulders, are opened to the sides. They are slightly curved. The palms face out.

▲ **Fourth position: The fourth *ouverte* (open) on the right and the fourth *croisée* (crossed).**

One arm remains in second position, the other is raised over the head.

◀ **Fifth position: The feet are crossed and lie flat beside each other.**

Both arms are held over the head and the palms face inwards.

At the Barre

Classwork always begins at the *barre* – a wooden rail fixed to the wall. The dancer does a series of exercises to warm the body, loosen the joints and make the muscles strong. Some of these exercises are shown here.

▲ *Plié* (left). This word comes from the French verb meaning 'to bend'. Every class starts with this slow bending exercise which relaxes the leg muscles. The knees are bent in line with the turned-out feet, until the thighs are parallel with the floor. *Pliés* are done in all five positions. Here is a *plié* in the second position. A *Demi Plié* (right) is a half *plié*. The knees are only slightly bent and the heels never leave the ground. This is a *demi-plié* in the first position.

◄ *Battements tendus.* These beating movements form part of several exercises. In a *battement tendu* the leg is extended to the front, side and back without lifting the toes from the floor.

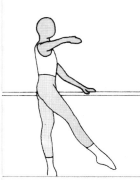
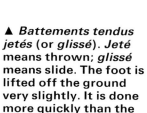

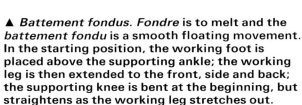
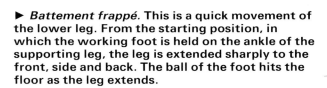

▲ *Battements tendus jetés* (or *glissé*). *Jeté* means thrown; *glissé* means slide. The foot is lifted off the ground very slightly. It is done more quickly than the *battement tendu.*

▲ *Battement fondus. Fondre* is to melt and the *battement fondu* is a smooth floating movement. In the starting position, the working foot is placed above the supporting ankle; the working leg is then extended to the front, side and back; the supporting knee is bent at the beginning, but straightens as the working leg stretches out.

▶ *Battement frappé.* This is a quick movement of the lower leg. From the starting position, in which the working foot is held on the ankle of the supporting leg, the leg is extended sharply to the front, side and back. The ball of the foot hits the floor as the leg extends.

▲ *Petits battements.* The working foot rests on the *cou de pied* (just above the ankle) of the supporting leg and moves quickly from front to back.

Grands battements. The leg, fully extended, is thrown up to waist level without bending the working knee or altering the hip line. This exercise can be done to the front, side or back and is used to strengthen the legs and loosen the hip joints.

▼ *Ronds de jambe à terre* loosen the hip joints. The toe traces a semi-circle on the floor: the foot starts in first position, moves through a *tendu* to the front, side and back, then closes in first position.

▼ *Ronds de jambe en l'air.* Here the working leg describes an oval in the air. This difficult exercise helps develop flexibility of the knee joint.

▼ *Développés.* This is a slow unfolding movement in which the working leg is extended to its highest point.

▼ Stretching. This exercise at the *barre* helps to develop leg muscles. Various examples are shown.

Centre Practice

Centre practice takes place in the middle of the studio, and for beginners consists mostly of repeating *barre* exercises without the *barre*. Later, more time is spent on *port de bras* (arm movements), pirouettes, poses, *adage* and *allegro*. *Adage* (an Italian word meaning slowly) is a sequence of slow exercises, and *allegro* (meaning quick) includes fast turning and jumping steps, and *batterie*.

Pirouettes. These are complete turns done on one leg. There are many different kinds of *pirouette.* One of the most common begins with a *demi-plié* in fourth position *croisée* and ends with a *demi-plié* in fifth position, during the turn, the working foot is drawn up with the toes just below the front of the supporting knee.

▲ *Arabesque.* This is a pose in which the dancer stands on one leg with the other raised to the back. There are various kinds of *arabesque.*

◄ *Attitudes.* This pose is based on a famous statue of Mercury. In the basic position the dancer stands on one leg with the other leg, bent at the knee, lifted behind. There are various versions of the pose.

▼ *Echappé* is a simple jumping step. The dancer starts with a *demi-plié* in fifth position.

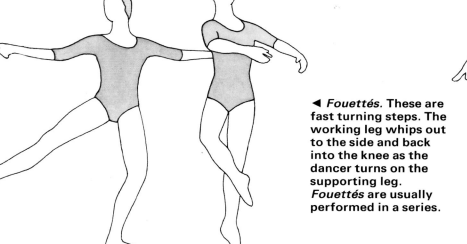

◄ *Fouettés.* These are fast turning steps. The working leg whips out to the side and back into the knee as the dancer turns on the supporting leg. *Fouettés* are usually performed in a series.

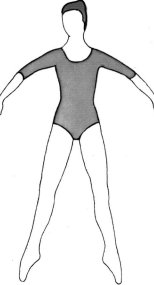

▲ *Assemblés.* These are jumping steps. The dancer brushes the working foot along the ground to the side, back or front while springing off with the other.

▲ *Soubresauts* (quick jumps) are straight jumps. The dancer begins with a *demi-plié* in fifth position, springs up with the feet stretched in the same position, and returns to a *demi-plié* in fifth position.

▲ *Changement de pieds* (changing the feet) is like the soubresaut, except that the feet change position in the air. This step is the basis of the *entrechat*.

▲ *Grand jeté. Jeté* is a jump from one foot onto the other; *grands jetés* are big jumps. The ability to rise high in the air is called elevation. Good elevation is particularly important for male dancers.

▶ An *arabesque penchée*.

19

▲ Point work. Girls usually begin point work after two years of class, when they are about 11 years old. In the beginning the exercises on *pointe* are performed at the *barre*; later more difficult work is done in the centre of the studio. One of the basic exercises on *pointe* done first at the *barre* then in the centre is the *echappé,* illustrated.

▲ Double work. Classes in *pas de deux* begin when students are about 15. The object of *pas de deux* is to show off the female dancer; the male's task is to support her, not just by physical strength but by under-standing the balance and rhythms of her body. In the illustration the boy is supporting the girl while she does an *arabesque allongée.*

► The grand *pas de deux* from the last act of *Coppélia,* danced by Noriko O'Hara and Dudley von Loggenburg in the London Festival Ballet's production. In this beautiful pose Swanilda is supported across Franz' knee and has her leg locked by his arm.

Modern Technique

Students who want to concentrate on modern dance go to special schools. As modern dance is constantly evolving, several different systems exist. The most popular is the Martha Graham technique.

At Graham schools, class is divided into three parts. The first part consists of floor work. The floor serves the same purpose as the *barre* – it aids balance. The student performs standard exercises in various sitting, kneeling and lying positions, as preparation for the rest of the class.

After floor comes centre practice, standing exercises that mostly involve the Graham technique's basic principle: the back as a source of movement from 'contraction and release' and the 'spiral'. Breathing out (contraction) makes the back and shoulders curve, breathing in (release) makes the back straighten. The spiral is the foundation of all turns: hips, waist, shoulders and head turn – or spiral – round the spine. The third section of class includes travelling steps, sequences across the floor, jumps and falls.

▲ These dancers from the Toronto Dance Theatre show how the angular, twisted body shapes used in modern dance are completely different from the flowing lines of classical ballet.

▶ A class in modern dance at the Ballet Rambert (above). In modern dance floor work replaces *barre* work.

▶ The Nikolais Dance Theatre in *Tensile Involvement*. Alwin Nikolais, an American choreographer, designer and composer, believes in 'total' theatre: all parts of a production are equally important. To make his productions as 'total' as possible, Nikolais creates the entire work himself.

◀ A game of poker provided the starting point for one of George Balanchine's ballets, *Card Game (Jeu de Cartes),* set to music composed by Stravinsky. Here members of the Stuttgart Ballet dance a new version arranged by their late director, John Cranko.

▼ In *Odine* (1958) (left) choreographer Sir Frederick Ashton gave Margot Fonteyn one of her most exquisite roles. He set the seal on the superb partnership of Margot Fonteyn and Rudolf Nureyev by creating *Marguerite and Armand* (1963). The short ballet is based on Dumas' novel *The Lady of the Camellias.*

▼ Literature is a frequent source of inspiration for choreographers. In 1869 Petipa choreographed a version of the Spanish classic *Don Quixote.* Balanchine produced a totally new presentation of the masterpiece. More recently, Karel Shook, co-director of the Harlem Dance Theater arranged the *pas de deux* from Balanchine's version for the group's repertoire. Here the *pas de deux* is danced by Joseph Wyatt and Elena Carter of the Harlem company.

The Making of a Ballet

The choreographer – the mastermind behind a ballet – decides on the story or theme, selects the music and arranges the steps and dance movements.

The starting point, the original idea, can be almost anything. Ballets have been inspired by the Bible *(The Prodigal Son)*, Negro spirituals *(Revelations)*, a game of chess *(Checkmate)*, by the US bicentenary *(Union Jack)* – in fact by all kinds of stories, events, moods and emotions.

All ballet stories have one thing in common: simplicity. As there are no words, everything has to be indicated through movement. So situations that normally rely on words are avoided.

Having settled on an idea, the choreographer then develops it into scenes and acts. With the scenario as the basic framework, the choreographer begins the unique task of creating dances. Choreographers have different methods of working. Some concentrate first on getting the feel of the ballet – music, theme, characters. Others study the music phrase by phrase, arrange each dance movement accordingly and go to the first rehearsal with the whole ballet planned in detail. Marius Petipa, the Frenchman who went to Russia and gave the world *Sleeping Beauty*, *The Nutcracker* and *Swan Lake*, liked to prepare dance patterns beforehand. He had a set of little figures like chess pieces, which he placed on the table in various positions. When a particular group pleased him he would note it for future use.

Most choreographers were once dancers, and are able to fully appreciate a dancer's reactions and abilities. They also know which steps are possible and which are not.

Music is a basic ingredient of ballet. Sometimes it even provides the initial inspiration. George Balanchine used Tchaikovsky's Serenade for Strings as a starting point for his ballet

▲ Inspired by the music and words of Mahler's *Das Lied von Erde,* Kenneth MacMillan created *Song of the Earth,* possibly his finest work, for the Stuttgart Ballet. *Song of the Earth,* about death as an inevitable part of life, has three main characters: the masked messenger of death, a man and a woman. The messenger claims the man, then returns with the man, for the woman.

Serenade. Frederick Ashton, inspired by Elgar's music, created a ballet about Elgar and his friends, *Enigma Variations.*

In other cases the idea comes first, the music second. The choreographer may ask a composer to write music specially for the idea or story. Petipa asked Tchaikovsky to write scores for *Swan Lake, Sleeping Beauty* and *The Nutcracker.*

Choreographers use their music in different ways. For some, the main purpose of music is

Writing it Down

For nearly five centuries there was no satisfactory means of recording dance. As a result, many great ballets were lost for ever. Others survived only by being pased on from one generation to the next. This century has seen the introduction of two efficient systems of dance notation. One was developed by Rudolf von Laban (1879–1958), the other by Rudolf Benesh (1916–1975). 'Labnotation' is widely used by modern dance groups, while the Benesh system, more suited to classical ballet, has been adopted by many companies. The sample of Benesh below is from *Rite of Spring.*

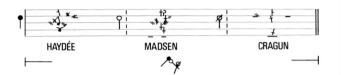

HAYDÉE   MADSEN   CRAGUN

▲ Joan Benesh teaching notation to pupils of the Royal Ballet School.

to produce a background atmosphere and they do not link it with the dancing. Others totally synchronize movement and music, and some make the choreography relate to the music without insisting that each step match each beat.

At rehearsals, the dancers themselves help create the ballet. This is particularly the case if the choreographer is one of those who arrives at the studio with an overall view of what the dancing is about, but with no detailed plan for each movement. The choreographer listens to a few bars of the music, thinks up some steps, tries them out and makes the dancer copy the movements. When the choreographer feels the movements are right, they move on to the next sequence. Creating a ballet is slow work. It can take an hour of rehearsal to produce one minute of dance. For a full-length ballet, the choreographer starts working with the principals a year or more before the production opens.

▶ One of the greatest-ever choreographers, Russian-born George Balanchine, trying a step with a dancer from his own company, the New York City Ballet. Balanchine died in 1983.

◀ Sir Frederick Ashton rehearsing members of the Royal Ballet in *Lament of the Waves*. The choreographer constructs the whole ballet.

▼ Sidney Nolan, the Australian artist, designed the costumes and scenery for the Royal Ballet's production of *Rite of Spring*. He is seen here painting the backcloth.

The designer begins work about a year before the ballet has its debut. He or she discusses the project with the choreographer before putting ideas down on paper. Most full-length story ballets need a lot of scenery. Before any of it is made a scale model is built on a miniature stage. Detailed plans are drawn up from a model and used to construct the real scenery.

On a smaller scale, there are props to prepare, items such as a horse for Kate and Petruchio in *The Taming of the Shrew*, or swords for Romeo and Juliet's warring families. Modern one-act ballets tend to use scenery and props sparingly, partly to concentrate attention on the dancing itself, and partly to save money. In Glen Tetley's *Pierrot Lunaire*, for example, the stage is bare except for a scaffolding tower.

In ballets in which there is little scenery, lighting often plays an important role. Changes in colour, in brightness and in range convey mood and atmosphere just as forcibly as painted canvas and wood do in traditional productions.

Costumes are an essential part of design. In a story ballet they help create character: a kilt

◄ Created specially for the cinema, *The Tales of Beatrix Potter* was choreographed by Sir Frederick Ashton and danced by members of the Royal Ballet. Much of the scenery was built larger than life to make the performers appear tiny.

► The opening scene of *La Fille Mal Gardée.* As dawn breaks over widow Simone's farmyard, the chickens wake up and greet the new day with a perky dance. This production by the National Ballet of Canada makes full use of scenery and costume to create the right setting.

▼ Members of the Toronto Dance Theatre in *Delicate Balance.* The symbolic arrangement behind the performers is very basic. Limited scenery and props are used in many abstract works. What little is used is often multi-purpose. A collection of ladders can be grouped to form a house, a tower or a cage.

for James in *La Sylphide*, a doublet for Romeo, plain cotton smocks for the peasant in *Giselle*. In abstract ballet they are used to project mood and theme. For Serge Lifar's pure dance work, *Noir et Blanc* ('Black and White'), the costumes mirror the title. The girls wear white tutus, while the men dress in white shirts and either black or white tights. However elaborate they look, costumes must be as light as possible yet hard-wearing. Light to allow free and effortless dancing; hard-wearing to survive hours of athletic movement and constant cleaning

Not all productions give the wardrobe so much work. Many of today's abstract ballets are performed in practice clothes.

A costume design by Alexander Benois for *Le Café* (Coffee) in a London Festival Ballet production of *The Nutcracker*. In the last act Coffee does an Arabian dance as part of the festival held to honour Clara and her Nutcracker prince.

▲ Piglets in a pas de deux from *The Tales of Beatrix Potter.* Their long snouts made dancing close together rather difficult!

◀ In 1948, Frederick Ashton choreographed his first full-length ballet, *Cinderella.* Here Robert Helpmann plays the superior, bossy ugly sister and Ashton himself the muddly one.

▼ A member of *PACT* Ballet from South Africa tries on her costume.

—A Ballet Dancer's Life—

▲ Long hours of rehearsal are frequently spent waiting. While the choreographer or dance master practises a solo with one dancer, the others must wait. They knit, read, or massage each other's legs to keep the muscles relaxed and flexible.

▲ A dancer's day must begin with class. On tour this can be difficult. Some theatres are so small that there is little room backstage. Here Ballet Rambert dancers on tour are doing classwork on the stage itself with the help of portable *barres*.

Dancing is not much like a job at all; it's more a way of life. A way of life that involves a lot of effort, time, discipline and routine.

The routine begins at about ten o'clock in the morning with class. All dancers – even stars – must practise every day to keep their muscles supple and maintain their technique. Class, which lasts up to two hours, takes place in a studio. In class, the dancers, wearing an assortment of clothes (tights, leotards, T-shirts, leg-warmers) do *barre* exercises and centre work under the direction of the ballet master. After a short break there follows four or five hours of rehearsal. The dancers, still guided by the ballet master, go through the ballet step by step. Rehearsals usually take place in studios, and often the soloists work in one studio and the chorus in another. But during the week before a first night the entire cast gets together with the orchestra and rehearse on stage.

Dancers have to arrive at the theatre well before the start of a performance. They need time to change, put on make-up and do some exercises to warm their muscles and loosen their joints. A performance means intense concentration and enormous physical effort, and when the curtain falls two hours later the dancers are very tired. At last they can go home to bed. They have reached the end of an average day, the sort of day that they have every day of the week, except Sundays.

Sadly, a dancing career does not last very long. It begins when a dancer joins a company at 17 or 18 and ends before he or she is 40. During the early years, dancers usually appear in the *corps de ballet*. It is rare for very young dancers to take the lead. As dancers gain experience, they play more important parts and, in time, they become soloists. A few reach the top: they become principals and dance leading roles.

Women dancers are generally at their best between 30 and 35, but three or four years later they have to retire. Men have to give up even sooner. There are exceptions. Great ballerinas like Ulanova, Markova and Fonteyn were still dancing in their fifties. But for most dancers middle-age means the end of one career and the problem of finding another. Some stay in the dance world as teachers, directors of ballet companies or even as choreographers. Others stay on the stage and take up acting. Others take ordinary, everyday jobs.

The outsider may wonder whether being a dancer is worth all the effort: such a long training and such hard work for just 20 years' dancing. This does not deter dancers. They are dedicated. And for dancers dedication is a must.

▲ A rehearsal on stage: choreographer Christopher Bruce goes through his very successful work, *Ancient Voices of Children*, with members of the Ballet Rambert.

▼ Inside the Maryinsky Theatre, Leningrad, home of the world-famous Kirov Ballet. The Maryinsky Theatre was built in 1860, but was not used regularly for ballet performances until 1889.

To a dancer, sore feet are a fact of life. Blocked shoes for *pointe* work are particularly painful. Dancers try to make things more comfortable by rubbing their feet with surgical spirit, stuffing cotton wool into the toes of the shoes, and by putting their heels – with shoes on – under the tap: the shoe shrinks, fits more tightly and so causes less friction.

Shoes are made from satin, which is not at all hard-wearing; to make them stronger, the toes are frequently fanned before use. Even so, ballet shoes have a very brief existence: a principal (a dancer with a leading role) can easily wear out two pairs of shoes in just one performance, while a chorus member, with much darning, could make a pair last a week.

Great Companies

The Royal Danish Ballet
The world's oldest ballet company is the Royal Danish Ballet. It is also one of the most important, thanks to Auguste Bournonville who was director of the company from 1829 to 1877. During that time he reorganized the company, introduced a different teaching method and created over 50 ballets. Among the best are *Napoli*, a folk tale from the Bay of Naples, and *Folk Legend*, based on a medieval Danish story. In his ballets, Bournonville always created exciting parts for male dancers, and Danish ballet remains famous for its male parts.

The Bolshoi Ballet
Bolshoi means great, and the Bolshoi Ballet is one of the largest and most important ballet companies in the world. In the days of the tsars this Moscow company took second place to the one in St Petersburg (now Leningrad), but after the 1917 Revolution, when Moscow became the new capital, every effort was made to turn the Bolshoi into the country's leading company. Today the Moscow company is the showcase of Soviet ballet. The Bolshoi became world famous for its superb dancing, and for stars such as Maya Plisetskaya, Mikhail Lavrosky and Natalia Bessmertnova.

The Royal Ballet
On the day on which the 13-year-old Frederick Ashton saw Pavlova dance, in the city of Lima in Peru, he vowed to become a dancer. He succeeded and became both a dancer and a choreographer. It was mainly as a choreographer that he joined London's new Vic-Wells Ballet in 1935. Working with its founder,

▶ Maris Liepa, as the tyrant Crassus, with members of the Bolshoi Ballet in *Spartacus,* one of the best known Soviet ballets.

▼ One of the Royal Danes' top dancers, Niels Kehlet, in *Etudes. Etudes,* an international favourite by the Danish choreographer Harald Lander, imitates a ballet class.

▲ Desmond Kelly and Marion Tait of the Royal Ballet in *Elite Syncopations,* a sparkling ragtime romp choreographed by Kenneth MacMillan. The ballet was first performed in 1974 and has become a firm favourite with audiences on both sides of the Atlantic.

Ninette de Valois, he made the Royal Ballet (as it is now called) into one of the world's greatest companies. During 40 years Ashton created masterpieces such as *Symphonic Variations, La Fille Mal Gardée, Two Pigeons, Enigma Variations* and *A Month in the Country.*

When Ninette de Valois retired as director Ashton took over, followed by Kenneth MacMillan, another gifted choreographer. The Royal Ballet has an outstanding repertoire. It also has a tradition of magnificent dancers including Margot Fonteyn, Robert Helpmann, Lynn Seymour, Anthony Dowell, David Wall, Wayne Eagling, Fiona Chadwick, Jennifer Penny and many others.

The Australian Ballet

When Diaghilev died, a new company, based in Monte Carlo, was formed to continue his work, the *Ballets Russes de Monte Carlo.* At the end of an Australian tour in 1939, one of the

▼ Members of the Australian Ballet in *The Merry Widow,* the first full-length work specially composed for the company. Adapted from the operetta by Franz Lehar, and choreographed by former Royal Ballet principal, Ronald Hynd, the ballet was first performed in 1975.

dancers, Edouard Borovansky, stayed behind and started his own ballet school and company. For 20 years the Borovansky Ballet entertained audiences in Australia and New Zealand with a *Ballets Russes* style repertoire.

After Borovanksy's death in 1959, the group disbanded but, two years later, many of its members came together again in the newly-formed Australian Ballet, under the leadership of Peggy van Praagh, a former director of Sadler's Wells. She was later joined by the Australian dancer and choreographer, Robert Helpmann.

Ballet Folklórico de Mexico
As its name implies, this company has its roots in the folk culture of Mexico. Its founder director and choreographer, Amalia Hernandez, was a ballet teacher with a great interest in the traditional life of her country. The ballet now has over 200 dancers. It combines modern and classical ballet with the rich dance heritage of Mexico.

Dance Theater of Harlem
In 1956, when Arthur Mitchell joined the New York City Ballet, he made history by becoming the company's first Black dancer. Mitchell trained as a soloist and became one of the company's star dancers.

In 1968 the Black Civil Rights leader Martin Luther King was assassinated. His death affected Black people everywhere. Mitchell was no exception. Inspired by the ideals of the Civil Rights Movement – equality for Blacks – he devoted himself to bringing ballet to his own race. He went to Harlem, New York's Black quarter, and started a school of classical dance. Two years later he founded the world's first Black classical ballet company: the Dance Theater of Harlem.

The Stuttgart Ballet
West Germany's Hamburg State Opera Ballet and the Berlin Opera Ballet are known internationally. But the really outstanding German

▲ Dancers of the Ballet Folklórico de Mexico in *Los Mayas.* Like much of Amalia Hernandez' work this ballet draws its inspiration from Mexican history and legend.

▼ Members of the Harlem Dance Theater in Mitchell's *Manifestations.* The ballet is based on the biblical story of the Garden of Eden.

company is the Stuttgart Ballet. Before 1960, the Stuttgart company resembled other provincial companies. Then John Cranko arrived and, within a few years, the Stuttgart Ballet had become world-famous. Cranko, a South African, was an exceptional choreographer. He created his first ballet in Cape Town and then moved to London to work for Sadler's Wells. Two of his biggest hits were *Pineapple Poll* and *Prince of the Pagodas*. At Stuttgart he brought in top dancers, founded a ballet school and built up an impressive repertoire. He died suddenly in 1973.

Nederlands Dans Theater

The Netherlands boasts three internationally known companies, all formed since 1945: the Dutch National Ballet, the Scapino Ballet and the Nederlands Dans Theater, famous for its adventurous – and sometimes controversial – productions. The Dans Theater, founded in 1959, aims to present contemporary work: each year it produces as many as a dozen new

▲ The Nederlands Dans Theater in the kind of contemporary production that is typical of its repertoire.

ballets. Most of these productions are specially created for the company, and are usually abstract (without a story) and set to modern music.

▲ During his twelve years as director of the Stuttgart company, Cranko added 50 new ballets to its repertoire including *Romeo and Juliet,* set to Prokofiev's music.

▶ Members of the Ballet Théâtre Contemporain in *Hopop,* a lively creation by Dirk Sanders, a Dutch choreographer.

Great Ballets

The Nutcracker

Danced to Tchaikovsky's sparkling music, *The Nutcracker* (1892) is performed more than any other ballet. The curtain rises on a Christmas party at the home of Clara and Fritz. Presents are handed out to the excited children. Clara is particularly delighted with one gift: a nutcracker shaped like a soldier. At the end of the party Clara and Fritz are put to bed and are soon fast asleep. Later the little girl wakes up and creeps downstairs to the drawingroom to play with her nutcracker. But strange things happen: the nutcracker grows bigger, then comes alive, and so does a regiment of toy soldiers. To Clara's horror, a regiment of mice, led by the ferocious Mouse King appears. The brave Nutcracker leaps to Clara's defence. A fierce battle rages. The Nutcracker and the

A London Festival Ballet production of *The Nutcracker.* This popular work is regularly staged by the company at Christmas. The Festival Ballet, founded by Alicia Markova and Anton Dolin in 1950, is world famous, especially for its superb full-length classical works. The company has recently changed its name to the English National Ballet.

Mouse King fight a duel. The courageous Nutcracker seems to be losing. Clara suddenly acts: she snatches off her slipper and throws it at the evil King; the Mouse King is distracted and the Nutcracker is able to kill him. The Nutcracker is transformed into a handsome prince and takes Clara on a magic journey through the Land of Snow to the Kingdom of Sweets. The Sugar Plum Fairy welcomes them and announces that a great festival of dance is to be held in Clara's honour. Then follows a wonderful entertainment: dancers from all

35

parts of the world perform for Clara and her Nutcracker Prince. As the dancing ends Clara feels terribly sleepy. When she wakes up she is alone at home with her Nutcracker doll. Was it all a dream?

Giselle

Giselle (1841) opens in a Rhineland village on the edge of a forest. Giselle falls in love with Loys, a peasant boy who has just arrived in the area. She has no time for Hilarion, a young woodman who wants to marry her. Hilarion, suspicious of the stranger, one day breaks into Loys' cottage where he discovers a nobleman's

▶ Dancers of the London Festival Ballet in *Coppélia*. Thanks to its delightful story and sparkling music, Coppelia is a great favourite with the public.

◀ Mikhail Baryshnikov (Albrecht) and Gelsey Kirkland (Giselle) with members of the American Ballet Theater in *Giselle.*

▲ A production of *Pineapple Poll* by the Royal Ballet. The music is by Arthur Sullivan. The ballet's lively light-hearted story is set in Portsmouth.

▲ *Petrushka,* danced by members of the Royal Ballet with Rudolf Nureyev (right) in the title role. Nureyev began his dancing career in Leningrad at the Kirov where he established himself as a phenomenal artist. In 1961 he decided to leave the USSR.

sword: Loys is really the Duke Albrecht. Meanwhile, a hunting party has stopped in the village for refreshment. The party includes Princess Bathilde, Albrecht's fiancée, and when Hilarion reveals Loys' true identity, Bathilde confirms it. Giselle is so shocked by the terrible news that she goes mad with grief and dies.

The scene changes to the forest glade where Giselle is buried. At night the forest is haunted by 'Wilis', the spirits of young girls betrayed in love. Any man who sees them is forced to dance until he is exhausted and dies. When Hilarion visits' Giselle's grave, he is surrounded by the ghostly spirits and dances to his death. Then Albrecht comes. Giselle herself is now a Wili, and Myrtha, the cruel Wili queen, orders her to make the duke dance until he, too, dies. But Giselle still loves Albrecht. She keeps him dancing until dawn, when the Wili power comes to and end. As dawn filters through the trees, the Wilis return to their

◄ Margarethe Schanne as the forest sprite and Henning Kronstam as James in the Royal Danish Ballet's production of *La Sylphide.*

▼ *La Fille Mal Gardée,* performed by the Sadler's Wells Royal Ballet (now called the Birmingham Royal Ballet). In the fields, the workers have finished the harvest and widow Simone is doing her lively clog dance.

graves leaving Albrecht alone, but alive – saved through Giselle's deep love.

Swan Lake

The greatest of Tchaikvosky's ballets is *Swan Lake* (1895).

The ballet opens with Prince Siegfried's 21st birthday: now that he has come of age he knows he must marry and choose a bride at a Grand Ball the next day. As dusk falls the depressed prince decides to distract himself by going hunting. Beside the lake he watches a flight of swans dropping down to the water. As the birds glide towards him, Siegfried is amazed to see the leading swan change into a beautiful woman. She tells him that she is Odette, queen of a group of maidens who have been bewitched by the magician, von Rothbart. Under his evil spell they are condemned to live as swans by day but become human

again by night. Siegfried falls in love with Odette and learns that the spell can only be broken if he promises to love her and no one else. Together they dance until dawn steals over the lake; then Odette, once more a swan, glides away.

At the Grand Ball, Siegfried hardly notices the young girls presented to him: all his thoughts are with Odette. Suddenly, two unexpected guests are announced: von Rothbart disguised as a nobleman, and his daughter Odile. By her father's magic Odile appears to be Odette and succeeds in captivating Siegfried. The prince asks her to marry him and swears his eternal love. Immediately von Rothbart and Odile reveal their true identity and, with mocking laughter, disappear in a cloud of smoke. Siegfried, distraught at having broken his promise to Odette, rushes to the lakeside to find the Swan Queen. There, he

La Sylphide

Created for Marie Taglioni by her father, *La Sylphide* (1832) was the first great romantic ballet.

The story takes place in a Scottish village where James, a young farmer, is about to marry a local girl, Effie. The day before the wedding, a forest sprite – the Sylphide – appears in James's house and the young man falls in love with her. He is torn between Effie and the Sylphide. While the couple prepare for the wedding a witch called Madge appears. She tells Effie that she will never marry James. In anger James drives Madge out of the house. But then the sprite succeeds in luring James into the forest.

In the forest James is blissfully happy and dances with the sprite. Yet disaster is near. Madge, determined to get her own back on James, makes a poison shawl which she gives to him. He hands the shawl to the sprite who puts it on. The evil spell begins to work: her wings drop off and she dies in James's arms. A wedding procession passes: Effie, thinking James gone for ever, has married his rival, Gurn. James collapses with grief.

begs her forgiveness and they are joyfully reunited. But their happiness is soon threatened: von Rothbart appears and says that Siegfried must keep his oath and marry Odile. To escape the magician's power, the two lovers plunge to their deaths in the lake. Their sacrifice breaks the spell: von Rothbart dies, the swan maidens become human again and Siegfried and Odette are united for evermore in a paradise beneath the lake waters.

▼ The London Festival Ballet in *Swan Lake.* The lyrical, sensitive movements of the *corps de ballet* form an exceptionally beautiful background to the soloists.

Index

Acknowledgements

Photographs: Australian Ballet Company page 32 *bottom*; BBC 30 *top*; Joe Bulaitis 34 *top*; Institute of Choreography 24 *top right*; Anthony Crickmay 5, 8/9; Jesse Davis 9, 12, 13, 21 *bottom*, 22 *top and bottom right*, 23, 24 *top left*, 28 *bottom left*, 31 *bottom left*, 33 *top and bottom*, 34 *bottom left and right*, 38 *top left*, 36, 36/37 *top*, 37; Zoe Dominic 11 *bottom*, 19, 20, 22 *bottom left*, 24 *bottom*, 25 *left and right*, 30 *bottom*, 32 *top*, 35, 36/37 *bottom*, 39 *top and bottom*; Danish Tourist Board 4; E.M.I. 26 *top*; 28 *top*; Giraudon 7; Malcolm Hoare 10/11, 21 *centre right*, 29 *left and right*; Mander and Mitchenson 8 *top*; Monarch Films 10 *bottom*; 8 *left*, 14 *top and bottom*, 31 *right*; National Ballet of Canada 27 *top*; PACT Ballet Company, South Africa 1, 3, 28 *bottom right*; Sadlers Wells Theatre 21 *left*, 26 *bottom*; Victoria and Albert Museum 7; Zefa 10 *top left*.